MACBETH: 12 AQA GCSE ENGLISH LITERATURE A STAR EXAM ANSWERS

Full mark A Star (Grade 9) Answers

By Joseph Anthony Campbell

Copyright © 2021 by Joseph Anthony Campbell. All Rights Reserved.

All rights reserved. No part of this book may be reproduced in any form or by any electronic or mechanical means including information storage and retrieval systems, without permission in writing from the author.

First Printing: May 2021.

For all professional enquiries, I can be contacted via email at Joseph@Agradeexams.com

CONTENTS

CONTENTS 1
The Quality Control System™ or how to get an A star!..2
Macbeth First Essay – The Witches...3
Macbeth Second Essay – The Supernatural..7
Macbeth Third Essay - Ambition...11
Macbeth Fourth Essay – Lady Macbeth...15
Macbeth Fifth Essay – Macbeth...19
Macbeth Sixth Essay - Banquo...23
Macbeth Seventh Essay – The relationship between Macbeth and Banquo..27
Macbeth Eighth Essay – The relationship between Macbeth and Lady Macbeth......................................31
Macbeth Ninth Essay - Macduff..35
Macbeth Tenth Essay – Lady Macbeth..39
Macbeth Eleventh Essay - Macbeth...43
Macbeth Twelfth Essay - Malcolm..47
Summary of GCSE English Literature Paper 1..50
Assessment Objectives...51
Timings..53
Approximate Word Count Per Question in English Literature Paper 1..55
Author's Note..56
About the Author...57
Limited availability for online and in person (in London) GCSE English tuition with me...........................58

By Joseph Anthony Campbell

THE QUALITY CONTROL SYSTEM™ OR HOW TO GET AN A STAR!

The Quality Control System™ is fourfold.

It involves:

1) An efficient summary of the examination paper.

2) A concise focus upon the Assessment Objectives in the exam and how to approach them.

3) Clear instructions on your timings and how long you should spend on each question. This is the most important point of fact in this fourfold system.

4) Further to point 3, the approximate word count per mark you should be consistently aiming for in each minute of your exam.

My students have applied all of the techniques of the Quality Control System™ I am providing you with to gain A stars (Grade 9's) in their examinations. You can replicate them by following the advice in this book. Following these rules has ensured success for my students in English Literature and their other subjects and it will do for you too! The Quality Control System is explained more fully at the end of this book.

MACBETH FIRST ESSAY – THE WITCHES

Read the following extract from Act 1 Scene 3 of <u>Macbeth</u> and then answer the question that follows.

At this point in the play, the witches are waiting for Macbeth and Banquo.

FIRST WITCH

Sleep shall neither night nor day
Hang upon his pent-house lid;
He shall live a man forbid:
Weary se'nnights nine times nine
5 Shall he dwindle, peak, and pine:
Though his bark cannot be lost,
Yet it shall be tempest-tost. -
Look what I have.

SECOND WITCH

Show me, show me.

FIRST WITCH

10 Here I have a pilot's thumb,
Wrackt as homeward he did come. [Drum within]

THIRD WITCH

A drum, a drum!
Macbeth doth come.

ALL

The weird sisters, hand in hand,
15 Posters of the sea and land,
Thus do go about, about:
Thrice to thine, and thrice to mine,
And thrice again, to make up nine:
Peace! the charm's wound up.

Starting with this extract, explore how Shakespeare presents the witches in <u>Macbeth</u>.

Write about:

• how Shakespeare presents the witches in this extract
• how Shakespeare presents the witches in the play as a whole

[30 Marks] (AO1 = 12; AO2 = 12; AO3 = 6) + AO4 = Spelling and Grammar [4 marks]

(50 Minutes Total = 40 Minutes Writing + 10 Minutes Reading Extract/Making Notes/Planning)

(600 Words Maximum per Essay = 15 Words per Minute)

Shakespeare presents the witches in this extract as awaiting Macbeth upon the heath. Their maliciousness is clearly evident in this extract. The First Witch states; "Look what I have." And the Second Witch replies with connotations of childish excitement

"Show me, show me!" The First Witch details her macabre property: "Here I have a pilot's thumb, wrecked as homeward he did come."

The witches are genderless and exist in darkness, and, when observed can vanish and become incorporeal. Shakespeare presents the witches as evil spirits of darkness. Their true desire, however, is for the temptation and destruction of Macbeth's soul. The Third Witch states. "A drum! A drum! Macbeth doth come."

Later in the scene, the witches greet Macbeth with a prophecy that he shall be king which has a great impact upon Macbeth. This sets an ominous tone for the remainder of the play by establishing a theme of moral confusion. Though the witches do not instruct Macbeth to kill King Duncan, they subtly plant the idea in his mind and guide him on the downward path to his destruction. Ultimately, Macbeth falls prey to temptation, whilst Banquo rejects it. This suggests that Macbeth can be easily manipulated and the witches take advantage of this flaw in him, which eventually leads to his demise. In this extract, when the First Witch states of an innocent victim that:
"Sleep shall neither night nor day Hang upon his pent-house lid; He shall live a man forbid:" It is presented by Shakespeare as a foreshadowing of what will occur to Macbeth throughout the rest of the play.

At the close of the extract the witches state: "The weird sisters, hand in hand, Posters of the sea and land,". This demonstrates their great supernatural power over the 'land' and the 'sea;' and here, the three witches, refer to themselves as the weird sisters. Their creation by Shakespeare was influenced by Holinshed's Chronicles, published in 1587 and King James VI of Scotland's Daemonologie, which detailed witchcraft and was published in 1597. When the First Witch discusses the creation of tempestuous storms at sea in the opening of this extract; "Though his bark (ship) cannot be lost, Yet it shall be tempest-tost" this is analogous to the North Berwick witch trials of 1590 which took place in Scotland. The witches involved, confessed to attempting to use witchcraft to raise a tempest upon a boat that both King James VI and the Queen of Scots were on.

Later in the play, in Act 4, Scene 1, the Witches, following orders from Hecate, produce a series of ominous visions through apparitions which are shown to Macbeth and which mock the hopes they awaken in Macbeth as they are really signs of his own demise. The interplay between reality and irreality is again shown as a theme of the witches by Shakespeare. In his meetings with the witches, Macbeth believes he is in control. However, the witches have the prophesies and thus the control. The witches have planned the two meetings in unison, both after this extract, 'Macbeth doth come' and in Act 4. It is their trap; he is the unaware outsider. He is arrogant but ultimately manipulated and submissive throughout the play, to the witches' suggestions.

The three witches represent evil, darkness, and chaos. Their presence throughout the play as a whole implies treason and impending doom. During Shakespearean times, witches were viewed as both political and spiritual traitors. Their existence within the play is located between reality and supernatural irreality. This leaves the audience to wonder: Do they control Macbeth's fate or merely influence it?

(600 words)

MACBETH SECOND ESSAY – THE SUPERNATURAL

Read the following extract from Act 1 Scene 3 of <u>Macbeth</u> and then answer the question that follows.

At this point in the play, after receiving The Witches' prophecies, Macbeth and Banquo have just been told that Duncan has made Macbeth Thane of Cawdor.

BANQUO

But 'tis strange,
And oftentimes, to win us to our harm,
The instruments of darkness tell us truths;
Win us with honest trifles, to betray's
5 In deepest consequence. –
Cousins, a word, I pray you.

MACBETH [Aside]

Two truths are told,
As happy prologues to the swelling act
Of the imperial theme. – I thank you, gentlemen. –
10 This supernatural soliciting
Cannot be ill, cannot be good. If ill,

Why hath it given me earnest of success,
Commencing in a truth? I am Thane of Cawdor.
If good, why do I yield to that suggestion,
15 Whose horrid image doth unfix my hair
And make my seated heart knock at my ribs
Against the use of nature? Present fears
Are less than horrible imaginings.
My thought, whose murder yet is but fantastical,
20 Shakes so my single state of man that function
Is smothered in surmise, and nothing is,
But what is not.

Starting with this moment in the play, explore how Shakespeare presents the attitudes of Macbeth and Banquo towards the supernatural.

Write about:

• how Shakespeare presents the attitudes of Macbeth and Banquo towards the supernatural in this extract
• how Shakespeare presents the attitudes of Macbeth and Banquo towards the supernatural in the play as a whole

[30 Marks] (AO1 = 12; AO2 = 12; AO3 = 6) + AO4 = Spelling and Grammar [4 marks]

(50 Minutes Total = 40 Minutes Writing + 10 Minutes Reading Extract/Making Notes/Planning)

(600 Words Maximum per Essay = 15 Words per Minute)

At the opening of the play, a major battle is won, due primarily to Macbeth and his lieutenant Banquo. Then follows a sudden appearance of the witches which poetically represents the supernatural. The hour of Macbeth's temptation is born of his victory and the powers of the supernatural are ready to strike. At this point, both Banquo and Macbeth are eager to hear the supernatural prophecies. While the two men wonder at these supernatural prophecies, the witches vanish, and Ross, informs Macbeth of his newly bestowed title: Thane of Cawdor. The first prophecy is thus fulfilled, and Macbeth, previously sceptical, immediately begins to harbour ambitions of becoming king. Macbeth gradually becomes fixated on the prophecy.

Macbeth states in this extract; "This supernatural soliciting Cannot be ill, cannot be good". This seeming contradiction reveals Macbeth's confused feelings through his use of questions and contrasting ideas. Fearful images are presented in this extract which demonstrate Macbeth's attitude to the supernatural "Whose horrid image doth unfix my hair". Macbeth is already devising "horrible imaginings" and thinking of committing regicide – despite the fact that this act will lead to his disintegration and downfall.

Shakespeare presents Macbeth in this extract as corruptible and as if his allegiances could shift dramatically; due to his state of internal and intense moral conflict – "nothing is, But what is not". The duality of Macbeth's feelings is clearly present in this extract as he ruminates upon whether he should believe what the witches have prophesied for him? These responses are the clear antithesis of Banquo's, who knows instinctively that the witches are supernatural forces of evil and should not be trusted. Banquo's firmer nature answers with clear insight "...oftentimes to win us to our harm these instruments of darkness tell us truths...to betray us in deepest consequence". Banquo is realistic about the "instruments of darkness" and through their deception; the "deepest consequence" of what they can lead him and Macbeth to. This illustrates the prophetic nature of what Banquo states and the witches' persuasive power. When we enter Macbeth's mind, we find in it the image of the murder to which he is tempted. Although the murder in his thoughts is yet only "fantastical", nevertheless it is there.

The supernatural is used by Shakespeare as a structural device that drives the plot and drives Macbeth. Macbeth's reaction is one of consumption and fixation. Macbeth, after this supernatural prophecy and with the aid of his wife, Lady Macbeth, commits regicide, despite his doubts and a number of supernatural portents, including a hallucination of a bloody dagger which leaves him so shaken that Lady Macbeth has to take charge. He attains the kingship of Scotland and thereafter lives continually in a state of anxiety and fear. Dramatic devices such as the appearance of the bloody dagger and the appearance of Banquo's ghost in Act 3, Scene 4 suggest how supernatural forces have overcome Macbeth.

Attitudes towards the supernatural and ideas about the soul and heaven and hell were prevalent in Shakespearean times. In terms of the dramatic context – the spectacle of the supernatural in the play would have been appreciated and understood by the audience and the themes of supernatural and natural are contrasted. Banquo acts naturally and does not act upon his prophecies whereas Macbeth becomes embroiled in the supernatural, becoming a murderer and a tyrant. Shakespeare presents Macbeth as an ambitious character who desires to control his own fate, rather than letting it be solely for the witches to decide but he eventually fully succumbs to the supernatural, returning to the witches for more prophecies; which he now believes completely.

(600 words)

MACBETH THIRD ESSAY – AMBITION

Read the following extract from Act 1 Scene 5 of <u>Macbeth</u> and then answer the question that follows.

At this point in the play, Lady Macbeth is speaking. She has just read Macbeth's letter telling her about his meeting with the three witches.

LADY MACBETH

Glamis thou art, and Cawdor, and shalt be
What thou art promised; yet do I fear thy nature,
It is too full o'th'milk of human kindness
To catch the nearest way. Thou wouldst be great,
5 Art not without ambition, but without
The illness should attend it. What thou wouldst highly,
That wouldst thou holily; wouldst not play false,
And yet wouldst wrongly win. Thou'dst have, great Glamis,
That which cries, 'Thus thou must do' if thou have it;
10 And that which rather thou dost fear to do,
Than wishest should be undone. Hie thee hither,
That I may pour my spirits in thine ear
And chastise with the valour of my tongue
All that impedes thee from the golden round,

15 Which fate and metaphysical aid doth seem
To have thee crowned withal.

0 1 Starting with this speech, explore how Shakespeare presents ambition in Macbeth.

Write about:

• *how Shakespeare presents ambition in this speech*
• *how Shakespeare presents ambition in the play as a whole*

[30 Marks] (AO1 = 12; AO2 = 12; AO3 = 6) + AO4 = Spelling and Grammar [4 marks]

(50 Minutes Total = 40 Minutes Writing + 10 Minutes Reading Extract/Making Notes/Planning)

(600 Words Maximum per Essay = 15 Words per Minute)

In this speech, Shakespeare demonstrates that Lady Macbeth is aware that her husband's temperament is "too full o'th'milk of human kindness" to achieve their ambitions. Lady Macbeth knows the moral weakness that is in him; that he be perceived in a positive way by others. If he had wished not to perform murder because it is wrong in and of itself, she may have honoured him for his courage. However, as Macbeth is ambitious for the crown, "Thus thou must do' if thou have it;"; it is murder that "thou must do", "To catch the nearest way." These are clearly ambitious statements from Lady Macbeth and she begins to plot the details of the murder in this speech. She recognises that she will have to give Macbeth her resolute qualities to achieve the prophecy and their ambitions i.e., she will – "pour my spirits in thine ear". Ambition here is clearly linked to both Lady Macbeth's rhetoric and manipulation.

Lady Macbeth is presented by Shakespeare as a pivotal character that drives the plot and the imagery within this speech states that Macbeth has what may be perceived as a feminine quality, as his 'nature' is "too full o'th'milk of human kindness". Through the soliloquy in this speech, Shakespeare adds dramatic tension and power. Lady Macbeth is a sole agent here; thinking and acting alone. This demonstrates her spirit of resolve and fixed purpose which she aims to instil in her husband. Immediately following this speech there is a message from a servant that Duncan will stay in their home that very night.

In Act 2, Lady Macbeth counters her husband's reservations, stating that he first set the wheels of murder in motion. Lady Macbeth says that she would dash the brains out of a baby's head, in order to challenge Macbeth's masculinity when he refuses to murder King Duncan; thus, belittling his courage and manliness. There is clear ambition demonstrated by Lady Macbeth here and her status and role in this relationship is clearly defined in the opening acts of the play. Ultimately, Lady Macbeth convinces her husband to commit regicide, after which she becomes Queen of Scotland. This suggests that Macbeth could be easily manipulated and that his wife, and the witches, take advantage of this flaw in him. Ideas about the supernatural witches and fate are alluded to by Lady Macbeth in this speech as a justification for regicide and her ambition;
"Which fate and metaphysical aid doth seem
To have thee crowned withal."
Macbeth is thus turned into a murderer by faulty rationalisations and manipulations. This is the beginning of his fall from greatness, as Scotland's primary defender. Lady Macbeth becomes her husband's executive and ultimately his executor, more resolute and consistent in her murderous intent. Contemporary reception to Lady Macbeth's behaviour may consider however that she is simply aiding Macbeth to carry out wishes that are merely his own, to her own detriment also.

The motivating role of ambition presented by Shakespeare in Macbeth appears to be omnipresent throughout the play and the consequences of ambition are explored by Shakespeare also. Macbeth may not have been initially predisposed to commit murder; but he has an overwhelming ambition that makes murder insignificant in comparison to not satisfying his ambitions. Macbeth's murderous and cruel actions seem to trap him in a cycle of increasing evil, as Macbeth himself recognises: stating that he is steeped "in blood" until his inevitable fall and Lady Macbeth's suicide. This ultimately signals the end of their terrible ambition, which is ultimately too large for their characters, in their unrightful roles as king and queen.

(600 words)

MACBETH FOURTH ESSAY – LADY MACBETH

Read the following extract from Act 1 Scene 5 of <u>Macbeth</u> and then answer the question that follows.

At this point in the play Lady Macbeth is speaking. She has just received the news that King Duncan will be spending the night at her castle.

LADY MACBETH

The raven himself is hoarse
That croaks the fatal entrance of Duncan
Under my battlements. Come, you spirits
That tend on mortal thoughts, unsex me here,
5 And fill me from the crown to the toe topfull
Of direst cruelty; make thick my blood,
Stop up th'access and passage to remorse
That no compunctious visitings of nature
Shake my fell purpose nor keep peace between
10 Th'effect and it. Come to my woman's breasts,
And take my milk for gall, you murd'ring ministers,
Wherever in your sightless substances
You wait on nature's mischief. Come, thick night,

And pall thee in the dunnest smoke of hell,
15 That my keen knife see not the wound it makes
Nor heaven peep through the blanket of the dark,
To cry 'Hold, hold!'

Starting with this speech, explain how far you think Shakespeare presents Lady Macbeth as a powerful woman.

Write about:

• *how Shakespeare presents Lady Macbeth in this speech*
• *how Shakespeare presents Lady Macbeth in the play as a whole*

[30 Marks] (AO1 = 12; AO2 = 12; AO3 = 6) + AO4 = Spelling and Grammar [4 marks]

(50 Minutes Total = 40 Minutes Writing + 10 Minutes Reading Extract/Making Notes/Planning)

(600 Words Maximum per Essay = 15 Words per Minute)

Shakespeare presents Lady Macbeth in this speech summoning to her aid those powers of evil which came unbeckoned to Macbeth "Come, you spirits…unsex me here". Her use of language suggests her desperation for power. Shakespeare also uses Lady Macbeth to influence the plot development. When Macbeth enters, later in the Act, the murder that is a thought for Macbeth has been determined resolutely in Lady Macbeth, as shown in this speech when she states, "…the fatal entrance of Duncan". At this point in the play, Lady Macbeth has significant power in terms of her relationship with her husband. Lady Macbeth could strengthen her husband in this time of weakness, and maintain his honour, however, when Macbeth is on the edge of this precipice, he is instead led to murder by Lady Macbeth; which ultimately ensures their downfall. Following the murder of King Duncan, Lady Macbeth receives power in terms of her status as a queen but in terms of being a powerful and effective character within the play, her role instead, significantly diminishes. When Macbeth is appointed king, he continues to murder and accrues more blood on his hands in order to secure his throne. He performs all of these further actions without consulting his queen. At the royal banquet, the queen is forced to dismiss her guests when Macbeth hallucinates and Macbeth, it appears, has now become entirely self-contained; and Lady Macbeths power almost completely diminished. In her final appearance in the play, she sleepwalks in profound mental torment. Through Shakespeare's use of unvarnished language which resembles Lady Macbeth's disordered mind, she reflects upon the blood on her hands and compulsively washes the spot from her hands. Powerless, now, over her hallucinations. Subsequently, she dies off-stage, apparently from suicide.

Ideas about power and how Lady Macbeth achieves it could arguably be perceived to have been obtained through supernatural means and her masculine approach in the play. The use and the effect of the imagery of the supernatural is demonstrated throughout this speech. Attitudes towards the supernatural and ideas about the soul and heaven and hell were prevalent in Shakespearean times. Lady Macbeth is a woman who desires to obtain supernatural powers and invokes evil spirits in this speech. She combines this with rejecting her femininity as shown in the following quotes, "unsex me here," and "Come to my woman's breasts, And take my milk for gall,". The fact that she conjures spirits shows similarities to the witches through using language to invoke spiritual powers to influence the workings of her woman's body and to make herself an instrument for bringing about murder. The witches are also depicted as defeminised and bearded. Witches could be perceived as an extreme type of anti-mother and Lady Macbeth states that she would dash the brains out of a baby's head in Act 2 in order to challenge Macbeth's masculinity when he refuses to murder King Duncan.

Ideas about the role of women and ideas about equality and status have changed considerably in 400 years and contemporary reception towards Lady Macbeth's behaviour in this speech and her actions elsewhere in the play may demonstrate her more favourably as a defiant, empowered nonconformist, and a clear threat to a patriarchal system of royalty. However, ultimately, she too may doubt her own powerful intentions in this speech and throughout the play as she appears perhaps aware of her powerlessness over her decency and perhaps femininity, as she states "Nor heaven peep through the blanket of the dark, To cry 'Hold, hold!'" This cry from heaven that she fears, is perhaps the voice of compassion contained within.

(600 words)

MACBETH FIFTH ESSAY – MACBETH

Read the following extract from Act 1 Scene 7 of <u>Macbeth</u> and then answer the question that follows.

At this point in the play, Macbeth is considering the reasons not to kill Duncan.

MACBETH

But in these cases
We still have judgment here; that we but teach
Bloody instructions, which, being taught, return
To plague the inventor: this even-handed justice
5 Commends the ingredients of our poison'd chalice
To our own lips. He's here in double trust;
First, as I am his kinsman and his subject,
Strong both against the deed; then, as his host,
Who should against his murderer shut the door,
10 Not bear the knife myself. Besides, this Duncan
Hath borne his faculties so meek, hath been
So clear in his great office, that his virtues
Will plead like angels, trumpet-tongued, against
The deep damnation of his taking-off;
15 And pity, like a naked new-born babe,
Striding the blast, or heaven's cherubim, horsed

Upon the sightless couriers of the air,
Shall blow the horrid deed in every eye,
That tears shall drown the wind. I have no spur
20 To prick the sides of my intent, but only
Vaulting ambition, which o'erleaps itself,
And falls on th'other.

Starting with this speech, explore how Shakespeare presents the character of Macbeth in Macbeth.

Write about:

• *how Shakespeare presents Macbeth in this speech*
• *how Shakespeare presents Macbeth in the play as a whole*

[30 Marks] (AO1 = 12; AO2 = 12; AO3 = 6) + AO4 = Spelling and Grammar [4 marks]

(50 Minutes Total = 40 Minutes Writing + 10 Minutes Reading Extract/Making Notes/Planning)

(600 Words Maximum per Essay = 15 Words per Minute)

Shakespeare presents Macbeth ruminating in this speech upon why he should not kill King Duncan and the consequences that may result from this act of regicide.
"Bloody instructions, which, being taught, return
To plague the inventor".
That if Duncan should be slain by his kinsman and his host, this is a double breach of trust.
"He's here in double trust;
First, as I am his kinsman and his subject,
Strong both against the deed; then, as his host,"
; and that he has been so gentle and so good a king,
"Besides, this Duncan

Hath borne his faculties so meek, hath been
So clear in his great office," that there will be a great outrage and outcry upon his murder; "Shall blow the horrid deed in every eye, That tears shall drown the wind".
It is worth noting that Macbeth does not hesitate because it is wrong to kill the benevolent and kind king, but because of the king's beneficence, this makes the chance of retribution upon Macbeth more likely; because Duncan's "...virtues Will plead like angels, trumpet-tongued, against The deep damnation of his taking off."
In the concluding lines of the speech, he states that there is no spur to do this but his ambition, "I have no spur To prick the sides of my intent, but only Vaulting ambition". Macbeth wishes to not perform this evil act, not because it is evil in itself, but because of the deeply negative consequences that could befall him. This speech reveals Macbeth's confused feelings through his ruminations.

Directly following this speech Shakespeare presents the entrance of Lady Macbeth. Her 'spur' is that of a fixed resolve against Macbeth's deliberation. Lady Macbeth answers firmly, as to her mind her husband has what may be perceived as a feminine quality; that his 'nature' is "too full o'th'milk of human kindness". She convinces him that he can kill Duncan and frame his attendants and thus escape consequence. This is the removal of the final barrier in Macbeth's mind to committing murder, as he is motivated by self-interest rather than morality.

Throughout the play as a whole Shakespeare presents Macbeth as physically brave and he also presents as distinctly that he is morally weak and easily influenced. He does not perform the right action as an end in itself but for the "Golden opinions" of others. In Act 1, Scene 3, the witches have given Macbeth a prophecy that he shall be king. This has a great impact upon Macbeth and sets an ominous tone for the remainder of the play by establishing a theme of moral confusion. Though the witches do not instruct Macbeth to kill King Duncan, they subtly plant the idea in his mind and guide him on his downward path to destruction. Shakespeare presents Macbeth's reaction to the witches' prophecy and his attitude in this speech as one of rumination and fixation. Ultimately, Macbeth falls prey to temptation. This suggests that Macbeth can be easily manipulated and the witches and Lady Macbeth take advantage of this flaw in him. It is their traps; he is the unaware outsider. He is ultimately manipulated and submissive throughout the play, to the witches' and Lady Macbeth's suggestions.

Macbeth is thus turned into a murderer by faulty rationalisations and manipulations and this is the beginning of his fall from greatness. As king, Shakespeare presents Macbeth continuing to murder and accrue more blood upon his hands in order to secure his throne until he is "in blood Stepp'd in so far" that he has no choice but to continue inexorably towards his inevitable and complete destruction.

(600 words)

MACBETH SIXTH ESSAY - BANQUO

Read the following extract from Act 3 Scene 1 of <u>Macbeth</u> and then answer the question that follows.

At this point in the play, Banquo is wondering if Macbeth killed Duncan.

BANQUO

Thou hast it now: king, Cawdor, Glamis, all,
As the weird women promised, and, I fear,
Thou play'dst most foully for't: yet it was said
It should not stand in thy posterity,
5 But that myself should be the root and father
Of many kings. If there come truth from them--
As upon thee, Macbeth, their speeches shine--
Why, by the verities on thee made good,
May they not be my oracles as well,
10 And set me up in hope? But hush! no more.

[*Sennet sounded. Enter Macbeth, as king; Lady Macbeth, as queen; Lennox, Ross, Lords, Ladies and Attendants*]

MACBETH

Here's our chief guest.

LADY MACBETH

If he had been forgotten,
It had been as a gap in our great feast,
And all-thing unbecoming.

MACBETH

15 To-night we hold a solemn supper, sir,
And I'll request your presence.

BANQUO

Let your highness
Command upon me; to the which my duties
Are with a most indissoluble tie
20 For ever knit.

Starting with this speech, explore how Shakespeare presents the character of Banquo in Macbeth.

Write about:

• *how Shakespeare presents the character of Banquo in this extract*
• *how Shakespeare presents the character of Banquo in the play as a whole*

[30 Marks] (AO1 = 12; AO2 = 12; AO3 = 6) + AO4 = Spelling and Grammar [4 marks]

(50 Minutes Total = 40 Minutes Writing + 10 Minutes Reading Extract/Making Notes/Planning)

(600 Words Maximum per Essay = 15 Words per Minute)

Shakespeare presents the character of Banquo in this extract as consciously distrustful of Macbeth: "Thou hast it now: king, Cawdor, Glamis, all, As the weird women promised, and, I fear, Thou play'dst most foully for't:" What was once a misgiving, in which Banquo had but little belief, is shown here at the outset of the third act as having grown into a suspicion, that is of little doubt. Banquo was there for their encounter with the witches and although he is unsure whether Macbeth committed regicide to gain the throne, here, he muses in a soliloquy (which is aside to the audience) that he is sceptical and suspicious of the new King Macbeth. He also remembers the supernatural witches' prophecy about how his own descendants would inherit the throne; "But that myself should be the root and father Of many kings". This perhaps makes him more suspicious of Macbeth's former actions in obtaining Kingship and of what he may do in the future. He then muses "May they not be my oracles as well, And set me up in hope?" and now, we find, that Banquo is not fully impervious to the witches' prophesies. His suspicions clearly remain too, as when he is aware that he is to presently be joined by, what for him, may be the perpetrator of the grievous murder of King Duncan, he immediately breaks off this line of enquiry and his soliloquy with,
"But hush! no more."

As Macbeth and his queen enter with an assortment of nobles and attendants, Macbeth hails Banquo to be the chief guest at their feast. Whilst Banquo is alive, Macbeth may feel that he must treat Banquo with great respect, for to him, he is the most dangerous of men, as we learn later on in this scene through Macbeth's soliloquy. Macbeth exclaims "Here's our chief guest." When Macbeth states "To-night we hold a solemn supper, sir, And I'll request your presence" his murderous thoughts lurk beneath his words of friendship. Banquo portrays loyalty to Macbeth with the servile words, "Let your highness Command upon me" and states at the close of the extract, with perhaps an inner cautiousness masked as obsequiousness, "my duties Are with a most indissoluble tie For ever knit". Although Banquo offers his respects to the new King Macbeth and pledges his loyalty, we are however, clearly aware of his suspicions through the preceding soliloquy. However, he is not consciously aware of the impending threat to his and Fleance's lives. It appears he is not yet ready or able to be fully and consciously aware of Macbeths murderous intentions and it is to seal his fate.

Shakespeare presents the character of Banquo in the play as a whole as an honest man, with a frank, strong nature. He is loyal to both Macbeth and King Duncan. Banquo is in a third of the play's scenes, as both human and ghost. He is of vital significance to the plot, yet has limited lines. Banquo, unlike Macbeth, is also sceptical of the witches; knowing the manipulations and temptations that evil can proffer. Due to "his royalty of nature" Macbeth sends murderers to kill Banquo and his son Fleance. When attacked, Banquo valiantly resists his attackers and sacrifices his life in order for Fleance to escape. He is both an oppositional force and foil to Macbeth as a human and a ghost, haunting Macbeth at the banquet in Act 3, Scene 4 and later on in the play, when he appears to Macbeth in a vision, wherein a long line of kings are descended from the noble Banquo.

(600 words)

MACBETH SEVENTH ESSAY – THE RELATIONSHIP BETWEEN MACBETH AND BANQUO

Read the following extract from Act 3 Scene 1 of <u>Macbeth</u> and then answer the question that follows.

At this point in the play, Macbeth is about to give his instructions to Banquo's assassins.

MACBETH

To be thus is nothing;
But to be safely thus. --Our fears in Banquo
Stick deep; and in his royalty of nature
Reigns that which would be fear'd: 'tis much he dares;
5 And, to that dauntless temper of his mind,
He hath a wisdom that doth guide his valour
To act in safety. There is none but he
Whose being I do fear: and, under him,
My Genius is rebuked; as, it is said,
10 Mark Antony's was by Caesar. He chid the sisters
When first they put the name of king upon me,
And bade them speak to him: then prophet-like

They hail'd him father to a line of kings:
Upon my head they placed a fruitless crown,
15 And put a barren sceptre in my gripe,
Thence to be wrench'd with an unlineal hand,
No son of mine succeeding. If 't be so,
For Banquo's issue have I filed my mind;
For them the gracious Duncan have I murder'd;
20 Put rancours in the vessel of my peace
Only for them; and mine eternal jewel
Given to the common enemy of man,
To make them kings, the seed of Banquo kings!
Rather than so, come fate into the list.
25 And champion me to the utterance!

Starting with this speech, explore how Shakespeare presents the relationship between Macbeth and Banquo in <u>Macbeth</u>.

Write about:

• how Shakespeare presents the relationship between Macbeth and Banquo in this speech
• how Shakespeare presents the relationship between Macbeth and Banquo in the play as a whole

[30 Marks] (AO1 = 12; AO2 = 12; AO3 = 6) + AO4 = Spelling and Grammar [4 marks]

(50 Minutes Total = 40 Minutes Writing + 10 Minutes Reading Extract/Making Notes/Planning)

(600 Words Maximum per Essay = 15 Words per Minute)

Shakespeare presents the relationship between Macbeth and Banquo in this speech through lines which represent Macbeth's thoughts upon and fears of Banquo as he dwells upon what the future may hold. "To be thus is nothing, But to be safely thus." He desires a security in his position as king that he does not feel and which is most likely unattainable. He focusses his feelings of insecurity on Banquo, "Our fears in Banquo Stick deep; and in his royalty of nature Reigns that which would be fear'd." Banquo is the chief threat as he perceives it, to both his position as king and his wife's position as queen. It is interesting to note that he speaks for both himself and his wife, as Lady Macbeth is left unaware of the plot to eliminate Banquo, that he is soon to execute. Perhaps he also notes that Banquo's "royalty of nature" is a quality he lacks as he explicitly states in this soliloquy, "There is none but he Whose being I do fear:" The evil prophesies of the weird sister witches have also poisoned his own "being" with the realisation of their predictions and the superior prediction and favour that was received by Banquo from the witches, that the "sisters...then prophet-like... hail'd him father to a line of kings: Upon my head they placed a fruitless crown". Banquo noted previously in this scene that Macbeth's "crown", "should not stand in thy posterity". This lack of posterity is mirrored when Macbeth states, "No son of mine succeeding."

Macbeth is jealous of Banquo and feels he undermines him, using a reference from another Shakespearean play i.e. "My Genius is rebuked; as, it is said, Mark Antony's was by Caesar" and this is further exemplified by the lines "He chid the sisters When first they put the name of king upon me,". Macbeth is clearly competitive in his relationship with Banquo, his fellow General and fears his descendants' inheritance of his crown and states that; "If it be so, For Banquo's issue have I filed my mind, for them the gracious Duncan have I murdered". To Macbeth's way of thinking, Banquo must die, and his son Fleance. Macbeth, is presented by Shakespeare here as a tyrant, in clear contrast to the "royalty of nature" of Banquo.

Shakespeare presents the relationship between Macbeth and Banquo in the play as a whole with Banquo as a foil and a contrast to Macbeth. However, at the outset of the play they fought side by side. In Act 1 Scene 2, a wounded soldier describes how Macbeth, Thane of Glamis, and Banquo, Thane of Lochaber, resisted invading forces. At Forres, whilst Macbeth had murderous intentions, Banquo was extolling Macbeth's courageousness to King Duncan. Throughout the play Banquo doubts the prophecies and the intentions of the witches; and resists evil whereas Macbeth embraces it. However, Banquo's motives are somewhat unclear. He never directly accuses Macbeth of murdering the king, even though he has clear suspicions as demonstrated in his soliloquy at the opening of Act 3. They appear to be bonded also through Banquo's premonitions of the oncoming darkness that precedes Macbeths murders. Banquo states at the end of Act One, "dark night strangles." And in Act 2 as Duncan goes to bed, he says: "in heaven, Their candles are all out" and finally he declares to his son Fleance, before he himself is killed: "it will be rain to-night".

During Macbeths soliloquy, presented here, the men chosen to be Banquo's assassins, await orders in darkness. However, Banquo's ability to live on supernaturally will become another oppositional force to Macbeth.

(600 words)

MACBETH EIGHTH ESSAY – THE RELATIONSHIP BETWEEN MACBETH AND LADY MACBETH

Read the following extract from Act 3 Scene 4 of <u>Macbeth</u> and then answer the question that follows.

At this point in the play, Macbeth has just seen Banquo's ghost.

MACBETH

Thou canst not say I did it: never shake
Thy gory locks at me.

ROSS

Gentlemen, rise: his highness is not well.

LADY MACBETH

Sit, worthy friends: my lord is often thus,
5 And hath been from his youth: pray you, keep seat;
The fit is momentary; upon a thought
He will again be well: if much you note him,

You shall offend him and extend his passion:
Feed, and regard him not. - Are you a man?

MACBETH

10 Ay, and a bold one, that dare look on that
Which might appal the devil.

LADY MACBETH

O proper stuff!
This is the very painting of your fear:
This is the air-drawn dagger which, you said,
15 Led you to Duncan. O, these flaws and starts,
Impostors to true fear, would well become
A woman's story at a winter's fire,
Authorized by her grandam. Shame itself!
Why do you make such faces? When all's done,
20 You look but on a stool.

Starting with this extract, explore how Shakespeare presents the relationship between Macbeth and Lady Macbeth in <u>Macbeth</u>.

Write about:

• how Shakespeare presents the relationship between Macbeth and Lady Macbeth in this extract
• how Shakespeare presents the relationship between Macbeth and Lady Macbeth in the play as a whole

[30 Marks] (AO1 = 12; AO2 = 12; AO3 = 6) + AO4 = Spelling and Grammar [4 marks]

(50 Minutes Total = 40 Minutes Writing + 10 Minutes Reading Extract/Making Notes/Planning)

(600 Words Maximum per Essay = 15 Words per Minute)

Shakespeare presents the relationship between Macbeth and Lady Macbeth in this extract with Macbeth initially exclaiming, "Thou canst not say I did it: never shake Thy gory locks at me" as he engages with the ghost of Banquo that is only visible to him. Lady Macbeth, desperately aiming to retain the guests, excuses Macbeth's passion as a fit to which he has been liable since 'his youth';
"Sit, worthy friends: my lord is often thus,
And hath been from his youth: pray you, keep seat;" and then with demanding whispers seeks to chide Macbeth into self-restraint; "Shame itself!". Lady Macbeth is presented here by Shakespeare as a scolding and re-assuring mother figure to Macbeth. We can discern here, that she has known him since his "youth" and she also states to him that "This is the air-drawn dagger which, you said, Led you to Duncan". We are therefore left to wonder if Macbeth has a history of hallucinations? Perhaps he has always had some schizophrenic symptoms? Lady Macbeth also undermines and attacks his masculinity, pointedly asking "Are you a man?" to which Macbeth retorts, "Ay, and a bold one". When an exasperated Lady Macbeth states "O, these flaws and starts," it brings into mind her words in the sleepwalking scene in Act 5, "my lord, no more o' that: you mar all with this starting."

In Jacobean times, the murder of King Duncan would be both shocking and treasonous and their lives would be forfeit if they were found out. It would be considered a disruption of the moral order of the divine right of Kings who were chosen by God, according to the biblical Old Testament. Therefore, a grievous act against the king was a grievous act against God. Lady Macbeth, therefore, may fear that Macbeth will go on to betray himself before all as the murderer of Duncan in this extract, and she hurriedly breaks up the banquet. Once together and now each apart from one another, they sink into despair.

Shakespeare presents the relationship between Macbeth and Lady Macbeth in the play as a whole with Lady Macbeth as the driving force for Macbeth's ambition at the outset of the play. She is acutely aware of the influence she has over him and her ambition is for both herself and for him. In the 'Great Chain of Being' of medieval Christianity, women were considered to be lower than and less powerful than men. Macbeth hints that Lady Macbeth has a masculine soul due to her ambition and in Jacobean times Lady Macbeth is perhaps quasi-dependent on Macbeth as a proxy for her desires for gender subversion.

Lady Macbeth has control of Macbeth and manipulates him, using persuasive techniques and emotional manipulation. He loves her, his "partner in greatness" and there is intimacy and affection between them but Macbeth is heavily influenced by Lady Macbeth and bends to her will. This is exemplified when Shakespeare uses the imperative "give," when Lady Macbeth demands "give me the daggers" to Macbeth, on the night of King Duncan's murder in Act 2 Scene 2. This implies that Macbeth has a subordinate relationship to his wife.

Lady Macbeth is strong, decisive and ambitious and Macbeth certainly appropriates this spirit throughout the rest of the play, acting alone and keeping his wife unaware of his further murders. Thus, Macbeth alone, becomes a tyrant. Macbeth and Lady Macbeth are presented by Shakespeare as needing mutual support before their act of regicide. However, afterwards, they share the crown in misery and lose both their sanity and their lives by the culmination of this Shakespearean tragedy.

(600 words)

MACBETH NINTH ESSAY - MACDUFF

Read the following extract from Act 4 Scene 3 of <u>Macbeth</u> and then answer the question that follows.

At this point in the play, Macduff has just been told of the deaths of his wife and children.

MALCOLM

Let's make us medicines of our great revenge,
To cure this deadly grief.

MACDUFF

He has no children. -All my pretty ones?
Did you say all? -O hell-kite! -All?
5 What, all my pretty chickens and their dam
At one fell swoop?

MALCOLM

Dispute it like a man.

By Joseph Anthony Campbell

MACDUFF

I shall do so;
But I must also feel it as a man:
10 I cannot but remember such things were,
That were most precious to me. –Did heaven look on,
And would not take their part? Sinful Macduff,
They were all struck for thee! naught that I am,
Not for their own demerits, but for mine,
15 Fell slaughter on their souls. Heaven rest them now!

MALCOLM

Be this the whetstone of your sword: let grief
Convert to anger; blunt not the heart, enrage it.

MACDUFF

O, I could play the woman with mine eyes
And braggart with my tongue! But, gentle heavens,
20 Cut short all intermission; front to front
Bring thou this fiend of Scotland and myself;
Within my sword's length set him; if he 'scape,
Heaven forgive him too!

Starting with this extract, explore how Shakespeare presents Macduff in <u>Macbeth</u>.

Write about:

- *how Shakespeare presents Macduff in this extract*
- *how Shakespeare presents Macduff in the play as a whole*

[30 Marks] (AO1 = 12; AO2 = 12; AO3 = 6) + AO4 = Spelling and Grammar [4 marks]

(50 Minutes Total = 40 Minutes Writing + 10 Minutes Reading Extract/Making Notes/Planning)

(600 Words Maximum per Essay = 15 Words per Minute)

Shakespeare presents Macduff in this extract at the exact moment that he receives the harrowing news of the murder of his wife and children. Although the news places Macduff in a place of profound grief, Malcolm attempts to use it as a rallying call to gain revenge against the murderer and thus balm their grief.
"Let's make us medicines of our great revenge,
To cure this deadly grief."
Macduff instead must remain in his profound despair, asking incredulously;
"-All my pretty ones? Did you say all?"
As Malcolm again attempts to steel Macduff's resolve for revenge against Macbeth, stating in blunt language, "Dispute it like a man", he perhaps learns that manhood is more than mere aggression when Macduff passionately informs him that he must also grieve for his loss. "I shall do so; But I must also feel it as a man". Macduff feels a profound sense of remorse for their murder exclaiming "Sinful Macduff, They were all struck for thee! naught that I am," and that their slaughter was "Not for their own demerits, but for mine,". Macduff left his family unprotected, and here, Shakespeare presents him as paying bitterly for it but also as a man who takes responsibility for his actions. He accepts the burden of his decision to leave his family and appears now to understand that his family was slain, "Heaven rest them now". When Malcolm again urges Macduff to take up arms with him against Macbeth, stating, "Be this the whetstone of your sword: let grief Convert to anger; blunt not the heart, enrage it." Macduff agrees that it is time to seek vengeance and retribution as the extract ends, "...front to front Bring thou this fiend of Scotland and myself; Within my sword's length set him;". Here, Shakespeare has Macduff dehumanise Macbeth with the use of the word "fiend".

Shakespeare drew mostly from Holinshed's Chronicles, written in 1587, for the character of Lord Macduff, the Thane of Fife. Shakespeare presents Macduff in the play as a whole, as a hero who plays a pivotal role. He is the avenging hero who rescues Scotland from Macbeth's tyranny. Macduff, like Banquo, serves as a foil to Macbeth and he is a moral figure. He represents a counterbalancing light in contrast to the ever-increasing moral darkness of Macbeth; his integrity contrasting directly with Macbeth's moral subversion. To Macbeth, manhood implies a denial of feeling, whilst Macduff demonstrates that emotional depth and sensitivity are part of what it means to be a man. The contrast between Macduff and Macbeth is also accentuated in their reactions to death. Macduff, reacts with a tortured grief, "But I must also feel it as a man" which indicates emotional sensitivity and contrasts starkly with Macbeth's nihilistic response to his wife's death in Act 5: "She should have died hereafter."

Macduff suspects Macbeth of regicide and flees Scotland and constantly examines the merits of his decision. However, he re-awakens his resolve and returns with a morality based on truth. Shakespeare presents Lennox referring to Macduff as, "some holy angel" and thus the play positions the characters of Macduff and Macbeth as good versus evil. Macbeth receives the retribution of rightful justice from Macduff at the end of Act 5, when they meet in battle and Macduff slays him. Macduff symbolically presents Macbeth's head, a token of justice, before Malcolm, and hails Malcolm as king and demands all to declare their allegiance to the rightful king. Thus, Macduff restores the rightful order of, and re-affirms his loyalty to, his motherland, "O Scotland, Scotland!" and avenges the murders of his wife and children.

(600 words)

MACBETH TENTH ESSAY – LADY MACBETH

Read the following extract from Act 5 Scene 1 of <u>Macbeth</u> *and then answer the question that follows.*

At this point in the play, Lady Macbeth's lady-in-waiting has asked the doctor to observe her mistress's strange behaviour.

LADY MACBETH

Out, damned spot! out, I say! --One: two: why,
then, 'tis time to do't. --Hell is murky! --Fie, my
lord, fie! a soldier, and afeard? What need we
fear who knows it, when none can call our power to
5 account? --Yet who would have thought the old man
to have had so much blood in him?

DOCTOR

Do you mark that?

LADY MACBETH

The thane of Fife had a wife: where is she now?--

What, will these hands ne'er be clean? --No more o'
10 that, my lord, no more o' that: you mar all with
this starting.

DOCTOR

Go to, go to; you have known what you should not.

GENTLEWOMAN

She has spoke what she should not, I am sure of
that: heaven knows what she has known.

LADY MACBETH

15 Here's the smell of the blood still: all the
perfumes of Arabia will not sweeten this little
hand. Oh, oh, oh!

Starting with this extract, explore how Shakespeare presents Lady Macbeth in Macbeth.

Write about:

- *how Shakespeare presents Lady Macbeth in this extract*
- *how Shakespeare presents Lady Macbeth in the play as a whole*

[30 Marks] (AO1 = 12; AO2 = 12; AO3 = 6) + AO4 = Spelling and Grammar [4 marks]

(50 Minutes Total = 40 Minutes Writing + 10 Minutes Reading Extract/Making Notes/Planning)

(600 Words Maximum per Essay = 15 Words per Minute)

Shakespeare presents Lady Macbeths entrance in this extract with the words "Out, damned spot! out," which recalls when Lady Macbeth stated that "A little water clears us of this deed" to Macbeth on the night of Duncan's murder in Act 2 Scene 2. Shakespeare presents Lady Macbeth in this extract as reflecting upon the blood, both literally and metaphorically, that has been on her hands; "Yet who would have thought the old man to have had so much blood in him?" She now has an imaginary blood spot on her hands and sleepwalks in a state of profound mental torment and imagines herself once again in the oppressive darkness that pressed around her on the night of the murder of Duncan. Her exclamation, "Hell is murky!" recalls that night when darkness gathered over the castle, and her place is now, in hell.

She recalls her former misguided confidence; "What need we fear who knows it, when none can call our power to account?" The gentlewoman proclaims "She has spoke what she should not, I am sure of That" which ironically brings into mind a remembrance of Act 3 Scene 4 when Lady Macbeth's fear is that Macbeth will go on to betray himself before all of their guests as the murderer of Duncan, and she hurriedly breaks up the banquet. Here, instead, it is Lady Macbeths unconscious that reveals what she has fought throughout the play to keep hidden and thus loosened her grasp on the power they have both tried to preserve. We observe her unconscious awareness and her knowledge of the further heinous acts by Macbeths' hand as she exclaims "The thane of Fife had a wife: where is she now?" and we can discern that the murder of Lady Macduff and her children and of Banquo now accuse her and have weighed and pressed down upon her guilty mind. She is not directly guilty of the subsequent murders after Duncan, but being guilty of one, the first one, she is to some extent, guilty of all.

Shakespeare presents Lady Macbeth in the play as a whole as suppressing her own feelings and aiming to protect her husband. She states in this extract, "No more o'that, my lord, no more o' that: you mar all with this starting". Her protective nature is again mirrored when she states somewhat maternally, in Act 3 Scene 4 to Macbeth "You lack the season of all natures, sleep" and in her statement to Macbeth in Act 2 Scene 2 when she states "These deeds must not be thought After" and Macbeth replies with: "Methought I heard a voice cry, 'Sleep no more!" This is a use of ironic foreshadowing by Shakespeare, as in this extract we can now discern that Lady Macbeth's own sleep has become tortured and her guilty conscience and the misery within her is now revealed explicitly. This ominous portent is clearly realised, culminating in the scene presented here by Shakespeare.

Ultimately, it is Lady Macbeth who coerced Macbeth into murdering Duncan in Act 2 Scene 2, instead of staying his hand and who led him over the edge of the precipice to their destruction and damnation. Shakespeare also assigns prose to Lady Macbeth in this extract, which is a Shakespearean device to display a characters' unbalanced mind, which is in contrast to the regular rhyme and balance of verse. Lady Macbeth is therefore the only principal character in Shakespearean tragedy whose last appearance has a clearly discernible prose structure rather than a verse structure. Later in this act, Lady Macbeth subsequently dies off-stage, apparently from her own hands.

(600 words)

MACBETH ELEVENTH ESSAY – MACBETH

Read the following extract from Act 5 Scene 5 of <u>Macbeth</u> and then answer the question that follows.

At this point in the play, Macbeth is in his castle at Dunsinane preparing to defend it.

MACBETH

I have almost forgot the taste of fears;
The time has been, my senses would have cool'd
To hear a night-shriek; and my fell of hair
Would at a dismal treatise rouse and stir
5 As life were in't: I have supp'd full with horrors;
Direness, familiar to my slaughterous thoughts
Cannot once start me.
[Enter SEYTON]
Wherefore was that cry?

SEYTON

The queen, my lord, is dead.

MACBETH

10 She should have died hereafter;
There would have been a time for such a word.
To-morrow, and to-morrow, and to-morrow,
Creeps in this petty pace from day to day,
To the last syllable of recorded time;
15 And all our yesterdays have lighted fools
The way to dusty death. Out, out, brief candle!
Life's but a walking shadow, a poor player,
That struts and frets his hour upon the stage,
And then is heard no more: it is a tale
20 Told by an idiot, full of sound and fury,
Signifying nothing.

Starting with this extract, explore how Shakespeare presents Macbeth in <u>Macbeth.</u>

Write about:

• how Shakespeare presents Macbeth in this extract
• how Shakespeare presents Macbeth in the play as a whole

[30 Marks] (AO1 = 12; AO2 = 12; AO3 = 6) + AO4 = Spelling and Grammar [4 marks]

(50 Minutes Total = 40 Minutes Writing + 10 Minutes Reading Extract/Making Notes/Planning)

(600 Words Maximum per Essay = 15 Words per Minute)

At this point in the play and in this extract, Shakespeare presents Macbeth as a man who has "… almost forgot the taste of fears;" as he has "…supp'd full with horrors;" and the torturous cry that he has just heard within has little to no effect on him;

"Direness, familiar to my slaughterous thoughts Cannot once start me." His thoughts and his actions are now slaughterous and dire screams are also now familiar to him.

When Macbeth hears of his wife's death he responds somewhat philosophically and perhaps nihilistically: "She should have died hereafter", then, unlike now perhaps, "There would have been a time for such a word". In "Tomorrow, and tomorrow, and tomorrow" Macbeth's words seem to express indifference. On one level, it is true and in line with a stoic tradition, that she would have died anyway, as we all will, "And all our yesterdays have lighted fools The way to dusty death." However, this may also signify a lack of feeling that has now accompanied Macbeths present state and a nihilistic view that he has come to adopt, as life is ultimately "...full of sound and fury, Signifying nothing". It is interesting to wonder whether there is some element of Shakespeare's own personal philosophy within these lines. Macbeth also continues on with his defence of his crown, leading the audience to wonder if Macbeths actions were, as now, always for his own benefit rather than for his and his wife's? Shakespeare also perhaps presents an inside joke with the lines "Out, out, brief candle! Life's but a walking shadow, a poor player," referring to the play being presented here indirectly. Macbeth is here, a "player" on a stage, in actuality.

Macbeths' physical courage is clearly presented by Shakespeare at the beginning of the play and is again marked here firmly at the end. Throughout the entirety of the play Shakespeare also presents Macbeth as ambitious. It is an ambition associated with usurping – and Macbeth also represents the Machiavellian idea that a ruler should appear well in public, presenting both strength and mental agility, and as we can see in this extract; to hold onto power until the bitter end. Macbeth commits regicide in Act 2 Scene 2 of the play and attains the kingship of Scotland but thereafter lives continually in a state of anxiety and fear. This solitary act leads to his disintegration and downfall as when Macbeth is appointed king, he continues to murder and accrues more blood on his hands in order to secure his throne.

Macbeth is a tyrant as a king and he also becomes progressively embroiled in the supernatural. Macbeths actions are in service of his ambition and he follows the powers of darkness, for his own ends. Shakespeare presents Macbeth as eventually fully succumbing to the supernatural, when he returns to the witches in Act 4 for more prophecies. At this point in the play, the witches had not yet dragged Macbeth down to the lowest depths and for the witches to achieve the complete perdition of Macbeths tempted soul, they must have him act with fiendish malice and this had not yet been achieved by the witches. After their meeting; Macbeth states wrathfully "And damned all those that trust them." Concurrently, he receives news that Macduff has fled to England, and then, through ordering the malicious murder of Lady Macduff and her children, the witches have now succeeded in fully corrupting Macbeth. He is presented by Shakespeare as the one who is made guilty by his own words. Macbeth's "trust" of the witches has now "damned" him fully.

(600 words)

MACBETH TWELFTH ESSAY – MALCOLM

Read the following extract from Act 5 Scene 9 of <u>Macbeth</u> and then answer the question that follows.

At this point in the play, Malcolm is making his victory speech at Dunsinane.

MALCOLM

We shall not spend a large expense of time
Before we reckon with your several loves,
And make us even with you. My thanes and kinsmen,
Henceforth be earls, the first that ever Scotland
5 In such an honour named. What's more to do,
Which would be planted newly with the time,
As calling home our exiled friends abroad
That fled the snares of watchful tyranny;
Producing forth the cruel ministers
10 Of this dead butcher and his fiend-like queen,
Who, as 'tis thought, by self and violent hands
Took off her life; this, and what needful else
That calls upon us, by the grace of Grace,
We will perform in measure, time and place:
15 So, thanks to all at once and to each one,
Whom we invite to see us crown'd at Scone.

Starting with this speech, explore how Shakespeare presents Malcolm in <u>Macbeth</u>.

Write about:

• how Shakespeare presents Malcolm in this speech
• how Shakespeare presents Malcolm in the play as a whole

[30 Marks] (AO1 = 12; AO2 = 12; AO3 = 6) + AO4 = Spelling and Grammar [4 marks]

(50 Minutes Total = 40 Minutes Writing + 10 Minutes Reading Extract/Making Notes/Planning)

(600 Words Maximum per Essay = 15 Words per Minute)

Shakespeare presents Malcolm in this speech after the deposing of Macbeth and the restoring of his rightful role as king. Restoration is a key theme in this speech and reunification. Malcolm states that we will "...reckon with your several loves, And make us even with you" and that former affections will thus be restored. During this final speech, he grants earldoms to Macduff and others, as he reclaims his birthright. "Henceforth be earls, the first that ever Scotland In such an honour named". There will also be a return for others as they call, "home our exiled friends abroad" who "fled the snares of watchful tyranny;". Malcolm delivers this speech and contrasts himself with the former regime, which produced "the cruel ministers" and the former tyrant Macbeth, who is simply referred to now as the, "dead butcher" and dehumanised. Macduff referred to Macbeth as a "fiend" in Act 4 and in this extract, Malcolm refers to Lady Macbeth as "his fiend-like queen,". Thus, both Macbeth and Lady Macbeth are dehumanised and presented by Shakespeare as personifications of evil. Malcolm represents the restoration of order in this extract and goes to great pains in his speech to demonstrate that his intentions are good, "...by the grace of Grace, We will perform in measure, time and place:". His speech concludes with him inviting everyone to his coronation. Malcolm appears here as a beneficent king, with Shakespeare using magnanimous language such as "loves", "even" "honour" "measure" and "grace". He and his allies are construed as forces for good and their eventual victory marks a restoration of moral order. Malcolm appears to be clearly aware that he has regained the throne and overthrown Macbeth through the support of those around him and marks this through his gracious speech. Contrastingly, he separates and sets himself in opposition to the former king, Macbeth and his Queen through the use of his terms for them and their rule, such as "tyranny", "butcher", "cruel", "fiend-like" and "violent". Shakespeare's use of descriptive contrasting language for each regime is clearly discernible throughout the presentation of this speech.

Shakespeare presents Malcolm in the play as a whole as both worthy of trust and patriotic. He is the natural heir to the throne as in Act 1, Scene 4, Duncan declares that Malcolm is his heir, "We will establish our estate upon Our eldest, Malcolm,". This act frustrates Macbeth and Malcolm becomes Macbeth's direct rival for the crown. Shakespeare based Malcolm on the historical king Malcolm III of Scotland, which he largely derived from an account in Holinshed's Chronicles (1587).

Malcolm, akin to his father, represents order and the natural progression of the throne. Malcolm is a guest at Macbeth's castle when Macbeth murders King Duncan and he subsequently flees to England. Shakespeare, however, presents Malcolm as having a firm resolve, as upon informing Macduff that his family was slain, he convinces Macduff to take up arms with him against Macbeth. Malcolm builds trust with Macduff and is presented by Shakespeare as a skilled statesman through securing the support of the Scottish noblemen and raising an army from England to reclaim his birthright from Macbeth's usurpation. Malcolm demonstrates leadership and compassion too when he consoles Siward after he receives news that his son was slain by Macbeth. He also demonstrates strategic skills, (which align with the final prophecy of the witches' apparitions to Macbeth) in his approach to Dunsinane Castle; when he obscures his forces. Ultimately, towards the end of the play, he is finally and fully recognised as king by Macduff, who proclaims to Malcolm, "Hail, King! for so thou art".

(600 words)

By Joseph Anthony Campbell

SUMMARY OF GCSE ENGLISH LITERATURE PAPER 1

This paper has a total of 64 marks.

There is 1 hour 45 minutes (105 minutes) for the exam (unless you have extra time).

Paper **1** is divided into **2** sections:

Paper 1 Section A: Shakespeare section. We are looking in this book at the **Macbeth option**. There are 12 examples of Grade/Level 9, A star essays in this book. (I will be writing further books on alternative Shakespeare options).
Section A = 34 Marks (including 4 marks for spelling and grammar)

There will be one task on the Shakespeare play. You will respond to a short extract from the play and demonstrate your knowledge of the play as a whole.

Paper 1 Section B: Nineteenth Century Novel (I will be writing further books on options for this).
Section B = 30 Marks

The best approach is to spend 50 minutes on each question in Section A and B - 40 minutes writing and 10 minutes reading the extract, making notes and planning. Ideally leaving yourself 5 minutes for basic corrections and checking at the end of the examination.

ASSESSMENT OBJECTIVES

There are **four assessment objectives** assessed in each English Literature examination: **AO1, (12 Marks) AO2 (12 Marks) AO3 (6 Marks) and AO4 (4 marks for Spelling and Grammar) and AO4 is allocated ONLY in the Shakespeare section of Paper 1.**

AO1 = Read, understand and respond to text (Macbeth) and the task set in the question. Use 4 to 6 quotations from the text provided and ideally 2 to 3 short quotes you may have memorised from the rest of the play (or memorise those that I have provided in my answers in this book on various characters/themes in the play).

AO2 = Analyse the language, form and structure used by a writer (Shakespeare) to create meanings and effects i.e., also mention 'Shakespeare' 4 to 6 times in your answer and how he presents characters/themes and creates meanings and effects.

AO3 = is the understanding of the relationship between the ideas in the text and the context/time in which the text was written and the context within which the text is set.

AO4 = spell and punctuate with consistent accuracy, and consistently use vocabulary and sentence structures to achieve control of the meaning you are aiming to convey.

The Assessment Objectives are not provided in the examination itself. However, I have provided which assessment objectives are being assessed in the practice questions in this book. It is important to be aware of the structure of how the assessment objectives are allocated in each question of the exam in order to maximise your opportunities to obtain full marks in each question.

TIMINGS

In the English Literature GCSE Paper 1 examination there are 64 marks to aim for in 1 hour and 45 minutes (105 minutes). Please allocate the correct words per minute per mark! Again, to re-iterate: The best approach is to spend 50 minutes on each question in Section A and B - 40 minutes writing and 10 minutes reading the extract, making notes and planning. Ideally leaving yourself 5 minutes for basic corrections and checking at the end of the examination.

If you have extra time allocated to you, just change the calculation to accommodate the extra time you have i.e., if you have 25% extra time (= 50 minutes per question = 12 words per minute and 20 words per mark) and if you have 50% extra time (= 1 hour per question = 10 words per minute and 20 words per mark) also equals a 600-word essay for each section on Paper 1. Again, please allocate within your time management 5 minutes for checking at the end of the exam but please **move on from the set question as soon as you have reached or are coming towards your time limit.** This ensures that you have excellent coverage of your whole exam and therefore attain a very good mark.

Similar to all the principles in this book, **you must apply and follow the correct timings for each question and stick to them throughout your exam to get an A star (Grade/Level 9) in your English Literature examinations.** Without applying this principle in these examinations (and to a large extent all examinations) you cannot achieve the highest marks! **Apply all of the principles provided in this book to succeed!**

APPROXIMATE WORD COUNT PER QUESTION IN ENGLISH LITERATURE PAPER 1

Now that you know what is on each examination, how the assessment objectives are assessed and the time allocated for each type of question; we come to what would be considered the correct word count per mark for each question. The primary principle though is to spend the right amount of time on each question.

In the answers in this book, I have provided the maximum word count for each answer which works out at **15 words per minute and 20 words per mark and therefore this equals a 600-word essay for each section on Paper 1**. If your answer has quality, this gives you the very best chance of obtaining the highest marks in your English Literature exam. Obviously, it does not if you are waffling however. (Please remember to answer the question set and to move on in the time allocated.)

I am aware that some students can write faster than others but all should be able to write 10 words per minute and thus a 400-word essay in the time (if they have not been allocated extra time). This is where conciseness is important in your writing.

My students and readers have applied all of the techniques of the Quality Control System™ I am providing you with; to gain A stars (Grade/Level 9's) in their examinations. You can replicate them by following the advice in this book.
Thank you for purchasing this book and best wishes for your examinations! Joseph

By Joseph Anthony Campbell

AUTHOR'S NOTE

This book will provide you with 12 crystal clear and accurate examples of 'A' star grade (Grade 9) AQA GCSE English Literature Paper 1 Macbeth answers from the Shakespeare section of the new syllabus and enables students to achieve the same grade in their upcoming examinations.

I teach both GCSE and A level English and Psychology and I am a qualified and experienced teacher and tutor of over 20 years standing. I teach, write and provide independent tuition in central and west London.

The resources in this book WILL help you to get an A star (Grade 9) in your GCSE English Literature examinations, as they have done and will continue to do so, for my students.

Best wishes,

Joseph

ABOUT THE AUTHOR

I graduated from the Universities of Liverpool and Leeds and I obtained first class honours in my teacher training.

I have taught and provided private tuition for over 20 years up to university level. I also write academic resources for the Times Educational Supplement.

My tuition students, and now, my readers, have been fortunate enough to attain places to study at Oxford, Cambridge and Imperial College, London and other Russell Group Universities. The students have done very well in their examinations. I hope and know that my English Literature books can enable you to take the next step on your academic journey.

By Joseph Anthony Campbell

LIMITED AVAILABILITY FOR ONLINE AND IN PERSON (IN LONDON) GCSE ENGLISH TUITION WITH ME.

Thank you again, for purchasing my book. I want you to be the first to know that I currently have some limited availability for GCSE English tuition. I am able to tutor in person, in London, or online.

Click or type the link/s below into your search engine to begin your journey of having one on one proven, expert tuition with me; in order to ensure that you reach the highest levels that you are fully capable of.

https://www.firsttutors.com/uk/tutor/joseph.english.psychology.philosophy-critical-thinking.religious-studies/

https://www.superprof.co.uk/joseph-english-teacher-and-writer-twenty-years-teaching-experience-proven-track-record-enhanced-dbs-check-the-update-service.html

My books have helped over 6000 readers and I am grateful to you for purchasing my book and to all who allow me to help them succeed.

I hope to be able to help you further in the future.

Best wishes,

Joseph

P.S. For all professional enquiries, I can be contacted via email at Joseph@Agradeexams.com

Printed in Great Britain
by Amazon